LITTLE KIDS FIRST BIG BOOK OF DINOSAURS

BY CATHERINE D. HUGHES
ILLUSTRATED BY FRANCO TEMPESTA

NATIONAL GEOGRAPHIC KiDS

WASHINGTON, D.C.

CONTENTS

How to Use
This Book
6

SMALL DINOSAURS 8

BIG DINOSAURS 40

GIANT DINOSAURS 72

GIGANTIC DINOSAURS 102

Parent Tips
120

Dinosaur Map
122

Glossary
124

Index
126

HOW TO USE THIS BOOK

Dinosaurs lived on Earth a very long time ago, before there were any people.

SMALL TO GIGANTIC
Dinosaurs came in all sizes. In this book you will find out about 52 small, big, giant, and gigantic dinosaurs. Some were small enough to hold in your hands. Others were bigger than elephants and taller than houses.

DINO FACTS
In each section, look for a drawing that shows the shape and size of the dinosaur. Next to the dinosaur drawing, you will see the figure of a kid who is four feet, six inches tall—about the height of a ten-year-old. That drawing will help you imagine how big that dinosaur was. In the same box, you'll see when the dinosaur lived and what food it ate.

GIANT

AMARGASAURUS HAD A NECK SAIL.

Amargasaurus may have used its **LONG TAIL** like a **WHIP** to **PROTECT** itself from attackers.

FACTS
WHEN IT LIVED early Cretaceous
FOOD plants
SIZE

This dinosaur's long neck and back were decorated with what looked like a sail. Stiff spines held up *Amargasaurus*'s sail.

No one knows for sure why *Amargasaurus* had the big sail. It might have scared away enemies. Or it may have helped keep the big animal cool.

SAY MY NAME: uh-MARG-uh-SORE-us

WHAT WE KNOW NOW
The text for each dinosaur uses information from scientists who study dinosaurs. These scientists are called paleontologists. This book tells you what paleontologists think now. Some information might change as scientists learn more about dinosaurs.

DINO ART

Because dinosaurs lived so long ago, before there were humans, there are no photographs of them. So an artist drew the dinosaurs you see in this book. The art shows what paleontologists think each dinosaur looked like.

FOR PARENTS

In the back of the book, you will find parent tips for dinosaur games and activities. Also, a world map shows where the fossils of the dinosaurs in this book were found. And finally, a glossary defines words found in the book.

Dig in for a lot more about amazing dinosaurs!

Some of the **SPINES** on the *Amargasaurus* were as **TALL AS A TEN-YEAR-OLD.**

How many dinosaurs do you see in the picture?

PRONUNCIATION GUIDE

This line tells you how to sound out the dinosaur's name.

IN THIS CHAPTER YOU WILL READ ABOUT 15 SMALL DINOSAURS.

SMALL
up to 15 feet long
(5 meters)

BIG
15 to 30 feet long
(5 to 10 meters)

GIANT
30 to 65 feet long
(10 to 25 meters)

GIGANTIC
more than 65 feet long
(25 meters)

Scansoriopteryx
(See pages 24 and 25.)

SMALL

Many **MEAT-EATING** dinosaurs had **FEATHERS**. No dinosaurs had **FUR**.

Have you ever seen a dragonfly? These insects also lived in the time of dinosaurs.

SMALL

MICRORAPTOR WAS A FEATHERED GLIDER.

Microraptor weighed less than four pounds. It is the smallest dinosaur in this book.

This little dinosaur had feathers and wings. It did not fly like a bird, but it could glide through the air like a kite.

Microraptor may have used the claws on its feet to climb high up into a tree. Then it leaped off, gliding through the air until it landed on the ground or a branch.

SAY MY NAME: MY-cro-RAP-tore

Dinosaurs lived **MILLIONS** of **YEARS AGO**. Dinosaur times are called the **CRETACEOUS, JURASSIC,** and **TRIASSIC.**

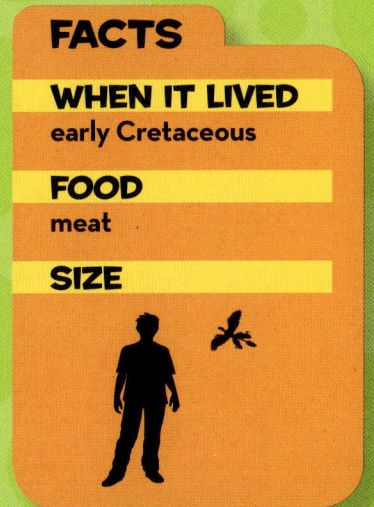

FACTS
WHEN IT LIVED
early Cretaceous
FOOD
meat
SIZE

SMALL

MICROPACHYCEPHALOSAURUS IS A MYSTERY DINO.

FACTS

WHEN IT LIVED
late Cretaceous

FOOD
plants

SIZE

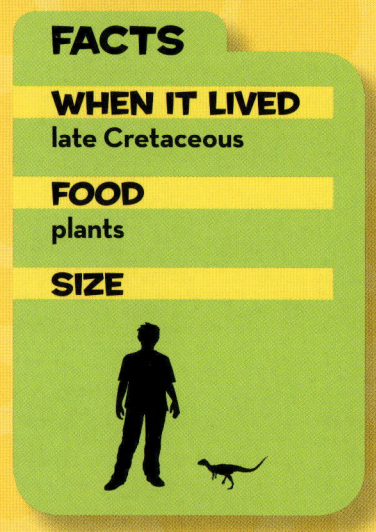

Scientists know very little about this mysterious dinosaur.

Micropachycephalosaurus may have lived in the forest. It could hide there from bigger animals that might eat it.

This small dinosaur probably sneaked around on the ground, hiding under plants. Maybe it climbed onto tree branches to hide in the leaves.

Micropachycephalosaurus is the **LONGEST** of all dinosaur **NAMES**. But it belongs to one of the **SMALLEST DINOSAURS!**

SAY MY NAME: MY-cro-PACK-ee-SEF-ah-lo-SORE-us

If you could have a pet dinosaur, what would you name it?

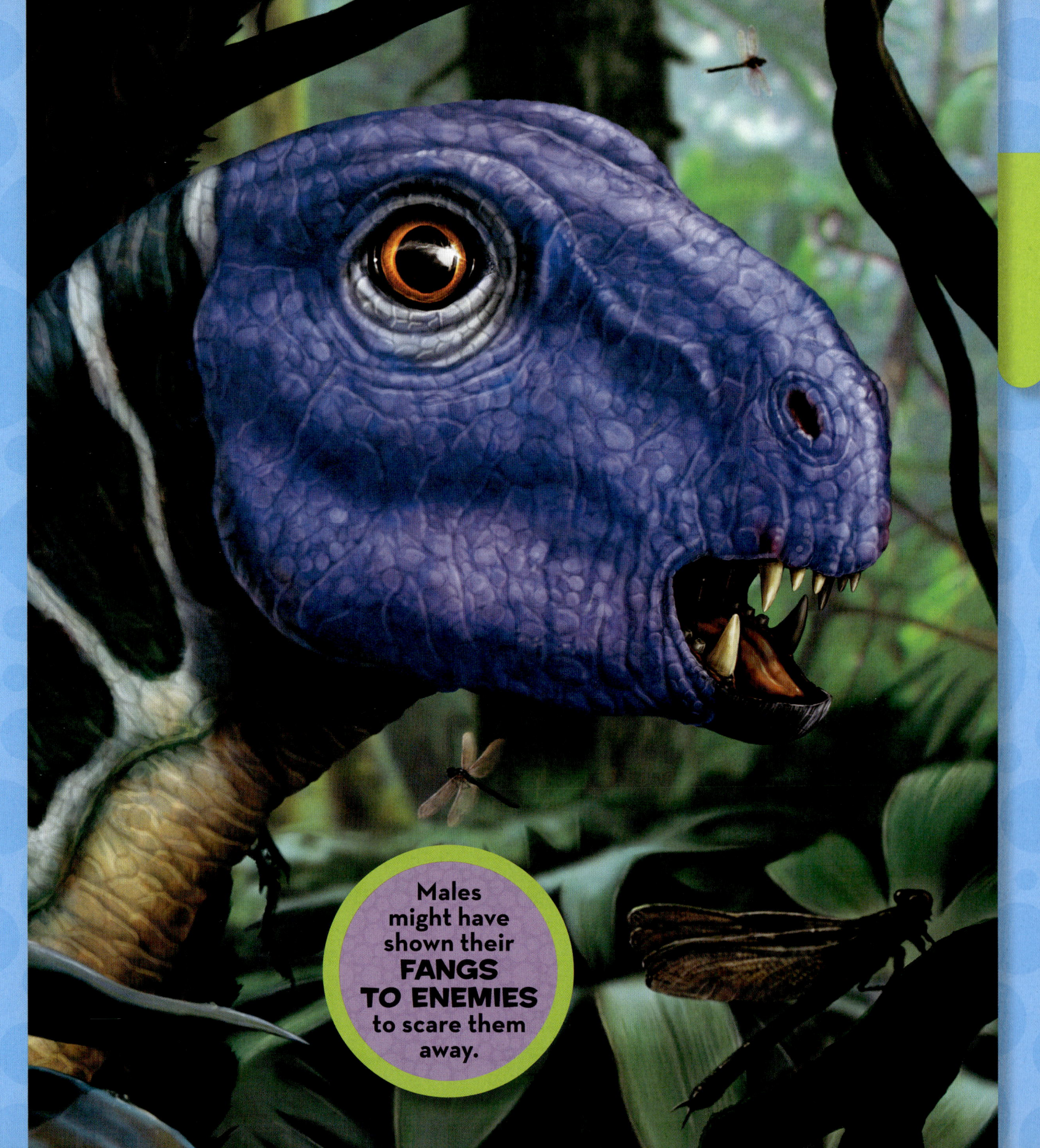

Males might have shown their **FANGS TO ENEMIES** to scare them away.

SMALL

HETERODONTOSAURUS HAD A TOOTHY MOUTH.

Heterodontosaurus had three different kinds of teeth.

The teeth in front of its mouth were small, sharp, and pointed. Those teeth were good for biting leaves.

Heterodontosaurus had bigger, flatter teeth in the back of its mouth. Those teeth were good for chewing.

Males had two long, fanglike teeth on each jaw.

How many kinds of teeth do you have?

FACTS
WHEN IT LIVED
early Jurassic
FOOD
plants
SIZE

SAY MY NAME: HET-er-oh-DON-toe-SORE-us

SMALL

OVIRAPTOR WAS A NESTBUILDER.

FACTS

WHEN IT LIVED
late Cretaceous

FOOD
meat

SIZE

Oviraptor looked very much like a bird. It had feathers. Like all dinosaurs, it laid eggs.

Oviraptor made nests for their eggs. They sat on the eggs to protect them.

Parents used their feathered arms to shade their eggs from the bright sun during the day.

SAY MY NAME: OH-vih-RAP-tore

Oviraptor **DID NOT HAVE TEETH.** These dinosaurs used their strong jaws to **CRUSH FOOD** such as lizards.

Where do you find shade when you play outside?

17

How many dragonflies can you count in the picture?

SMALL

COMPSOGNATHUS WAS A LIZARD HUNTER.

Some dinosaurs hunted other animals. These meat-eaters are called predators. The animals they hunt are called prey.

Compsognathus was a predator. It ran quickly on its two hind legs to catch its prey—lizards, insects, and other small animals.

Compsognathus was about the SIZE OF A TURKEY.

FACTS

WHEN IT LIVED
late Jurassic

FOOD
meat

SIZE

SAY MY NAME: KOMP-sog-NAH-thus

SMALL

ARCHAEORNITHOMIMUS WAS A SPEEDY RUNNER.

Archaeornithomimus had long, strong legs. It could run very fast.

Some kinds of dinosaurs ate both meat and plants. Animals that eat both are called omnivores.

This speedy runner was an omnivore. It ate fruit, leaves, eggs, and small animals.

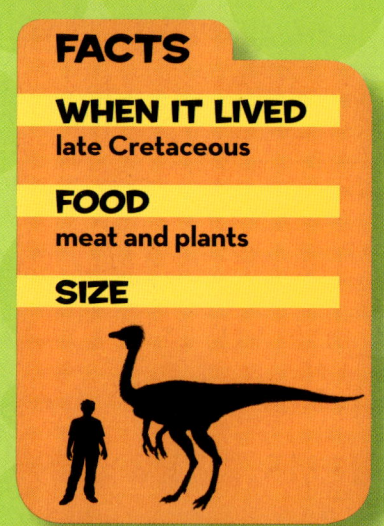

FACTS

WHEN IT LIVED
late Cretaceous

FOOD
meat and plants

SIZE

What is your favorite dinner?

SAY MY NAME: AHR-kee-or-NI-thoh-MIME-us

This **DINOSAUR** had **NO TEETH**.

21

Can you draw a picture of a dinosaur with bumpy skin?

Some dinosaurs may have lived to be **100 YEARS OLD.**

SMALL

SCUTELLOSAURUS WAS AN ARMORED DINO.

Scutellosaurus had more than 300 little bumps in its skin. Those bumps were hard little bones.

The bones helped protect the plant-eater. It was as if it had a suit of armor, like a knight.

Scutellosaurus ran on its hind legs. It had a very long tail. The tail helped it balance.

SAY MY NAME: skoo-**TELL**-oh-**SORE**-us

Scutellosaurus was one species, or kind, of dinosaur. Many **SPECIES** of **DINOSAURS** lived at the same time.

FACTS

WHEN IT LIVED
early Jurassic

FOOD
plants

SIZE

SMALL

SCANSORIOPTERYX WAS A WINGED CLIMBER.

This tiny dinosaur had feathers and could glide. It had long fingers with strong claws. The claws helped it climb trees.

Up in the treetops, this dinosaur could hunt for insects to eat. Maybe it ate beetles like the one crawling near the *Scansoriopteryx* in the picture.

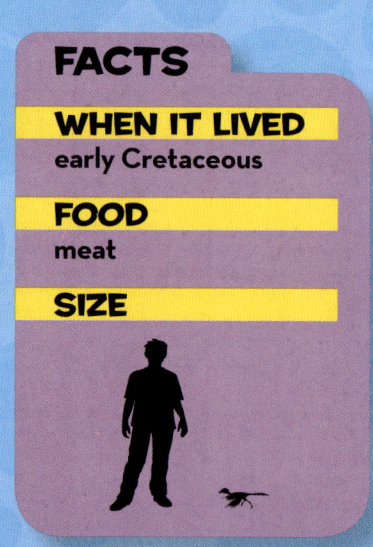

FACTS

WHEN IT LIVED
early Cretaceous

FOOD
meat

SIZE

Which other dinosaurs in this book could glide? (HINT: Look on pages 10 and 28.)

SAY MY NAME: SCAN-sore-ee-**OP**-tore-icks

This dinosaur may have used its **CLAWS** to **PULL OUT BUGS** from under tree bark.

PALEONTOLOGISTS are scientists who study **DINOSAURS.**

25

Paleontologists learn about dinosaurs by **DIGGING** up **BONES, TEETH,** and **FOOTPRINTS** that the dinosaurs left behind.

Have you ever found something while digging in dirt or sand?

SMALL

PSITTACOSAURUS HAD A PARROT BEAK.

Psittacosaurus did not have any teeth in the front of its mouth. It used its beak like scissors to cut through plants. It did have teeth in the back of its jaws that it used for chewing.

There were dinosaurs on Earth for millions of years. Some kinds, such as *Psittacosaurus*, lived in deserts, where it was very dry. Others lived in forests. Some lived where the weather was hot, and others where it was cold.

SAY MY NAME: SIT-ah-co-SORE-us

Some dinosaur **PARTS** hardened over time and became **FOSSILS**.

FACTS

WHEN IT LIVED
early Cretaceous

FOOD
plants

SIZE

SMALL

ARCHAEOPTERYX WAS AN EARLY BIRD.

Archaeopteryx is the first bird that paleontologists have found. It was a link, or connection, between dinosaurs and birds.

Archaeopteryx was a dinosaur *and* a bird. Over millions of years, the first birds and all their babies evolved, or changed.

Little by little they began to look more like the birds you see today.

FACTS

WHEN IT LIVED
late Jurassic

FOOD
meat

SIZE

The **BIRDS** you see every day are some of the closest living relatives of the **DINOSAURS**.

SAY MY NAME: ARK-ee-OP-turr-icks

No one knows whether *Archaeopteryx* could actually fly or could only **GLIDE.**

What kinds of birds do you see in your neighborhood?

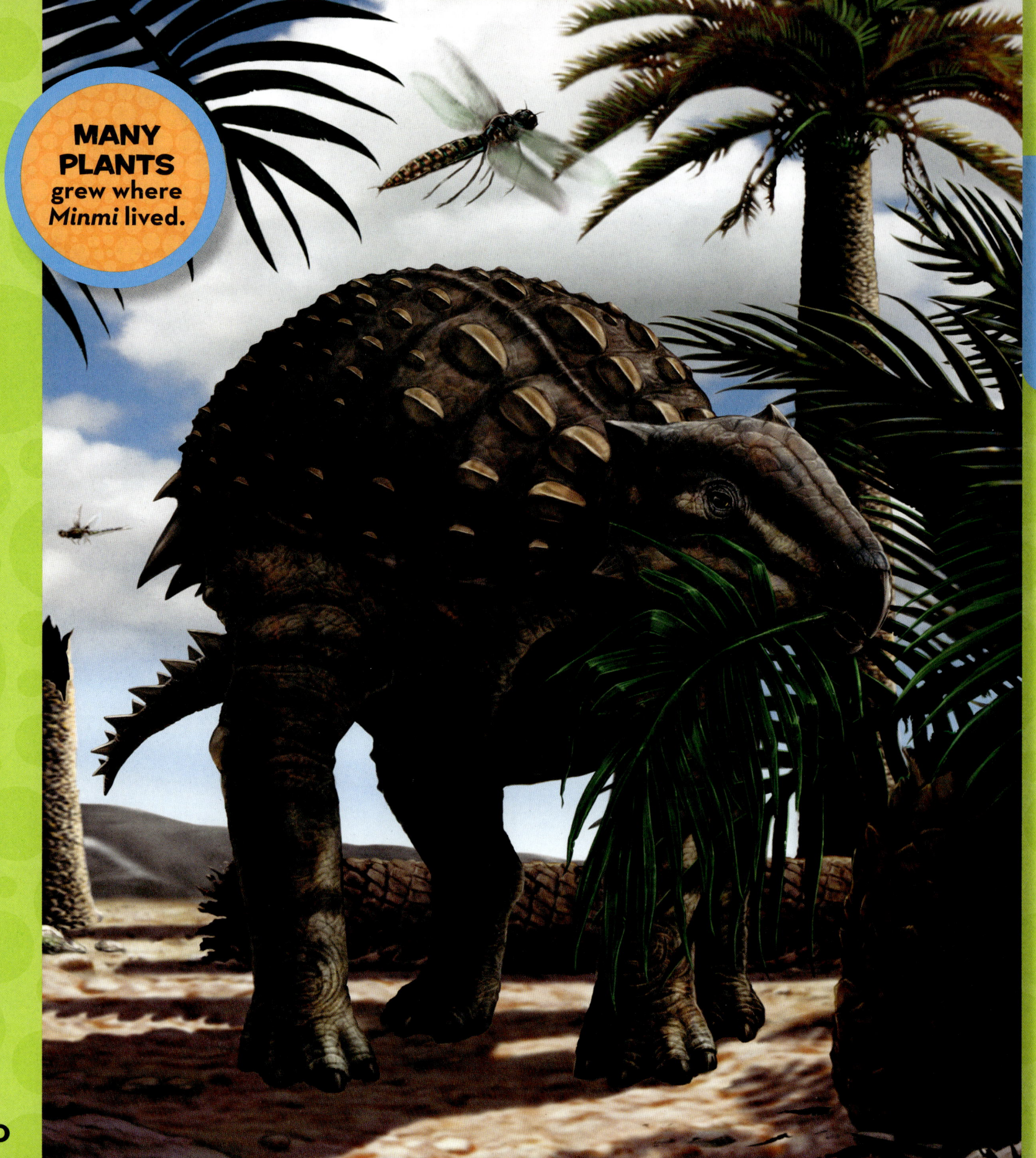

MANY PLANTS grew where *Minmi* lived.

SMALL

MINMI WAS A SLOW MOVER.

Minmi moved slowly. Its tough body was covered with hard armor. It even had armor that grew in the skin on its stomach.

Minmi had small, sharp teeth that it used to bite off the plants it ate. It probably swallowed fruits and seeds whole.

There were **MORE PLANT-EATING** dinosaurs **THAN MEAT-EATING** dinosaurs.

FACTS
WHEN IT LIVED
early Cretaceous
FOOD
plants
SIZE

Can you name some fruits that you like to eat?

SAY MY NAME: MIN-mee

SMALL

BUITRERAPTOR WAS AN INSECT CHASER.

Buitreraptor had small teeth. Its teeth were too small to use for hunting big animals. This dinosaur caught insects, lizards, and other small animals to eat.

Buitreraptor **PROBABLY** used its **LONG, SHARP CLAWS INSTEAD** of its **TEETH** to defend itself.

FACTS
WHEN IT LIVED late Cretaceous
FOOD meat
SIZE

Buitreraptor is one of many kinds of dinosaur fossils found in Argentina, South America. Other countries where many dinosaur fossils were found include the United States, Canada, China, Mongolia, Niger, and South Africa.

SAY MY NAME: BWEE-tre-RAP-tore

Can you think of any of today's animals that eat insects?

What color would you want to be if you were a dinosaur?

SMALL

LEAELLYNASAURA HAD BIG EYES.

This small plant-eater lived near the South Pole, where it was dark and cold part of the year.

Leaellynasaura may have dug burrows to curl up in to stay warm.

Scientists do not know for sure what colors dinosaurs were, but they can make good guesses. They think some dinosaurs may have been very colorful.

Some new species of dinosaurs were **DISCOVERED** by **CHILDREN** who found fossils!

FACTS

WHEN IT LIVED
early Cretaceous

FOOD
plants

SIZE

SAY MY NAME: lee-EL-in-a-SORE-a

SMALL

HUAYANGOSAURUS HAD A SPIKY BACK.

Large **MEAT-EATING DINOSAURS LIVED** at the **SAME TIME** as this **SPIKY-BACKED PLANT-EATER.**

The pointy spikes on *Huayangosaurus*'s body may have been protection against predators. The two big spikes on its back might have stopped taller meat-eaters from biting this dinosaur.

Huayangosaurus also had flatter spikes, called plates, that grew along its whole back.

FACTS

WHEN IT LIVED
middle Jurassic

FOOD
plants

SIZE

SAY MY NAME: hwah-YANG-oh-SORE-us

Flying reptiles called **PTEROSAURS** (TER-uh-sores) **LIVED IN THE TIME** of dinosaurs.

Can you find three pterosaurs flying near this *Huayangosaurus*?

Struthiomimus means **"OSTRICH MIMIC."** This dinosaur looks a little like an ostrich.

Have you ever seen an ostrich?

38

SMALL

STRUTHIOMIMUS WAS QUICK ON ITS FEET.

Struthiomimus was one of the fastest runners of all dinosaurs. Its legs were long and strong. It ran faster than any human.

The dinosaur had a small head and a long neck and tail. Its stiff tail helped *Struthiomimus* keep its balance as it ran.

Scientists think *Struthiomimus* was omnivorous. It may have eaten plants as well as small animals such as lizards.

FACTS

WHEN IT LIVED
late Cretaceous

FOOD
meat and plants

SIZE

SAY MY NAME: strooth-ee-oh-MY-muss

IN THIS CHAPTER YOU WILL READ ABOUT 15 BIG DINOSAURS.

SMALL
up to 15 feet long
(5 meters)

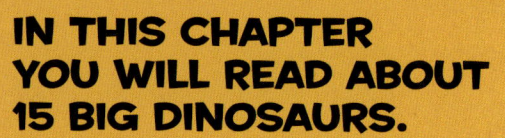

BIG
15 to 30 feet long
(5 to 10 meters)

GIANT
30 to 65 feet long
(10 to 25 meters)

GIGANTIC
more than 65 feet long
(25 meters)

Triceratops
(See pages 54 and 55.)

40

BIG

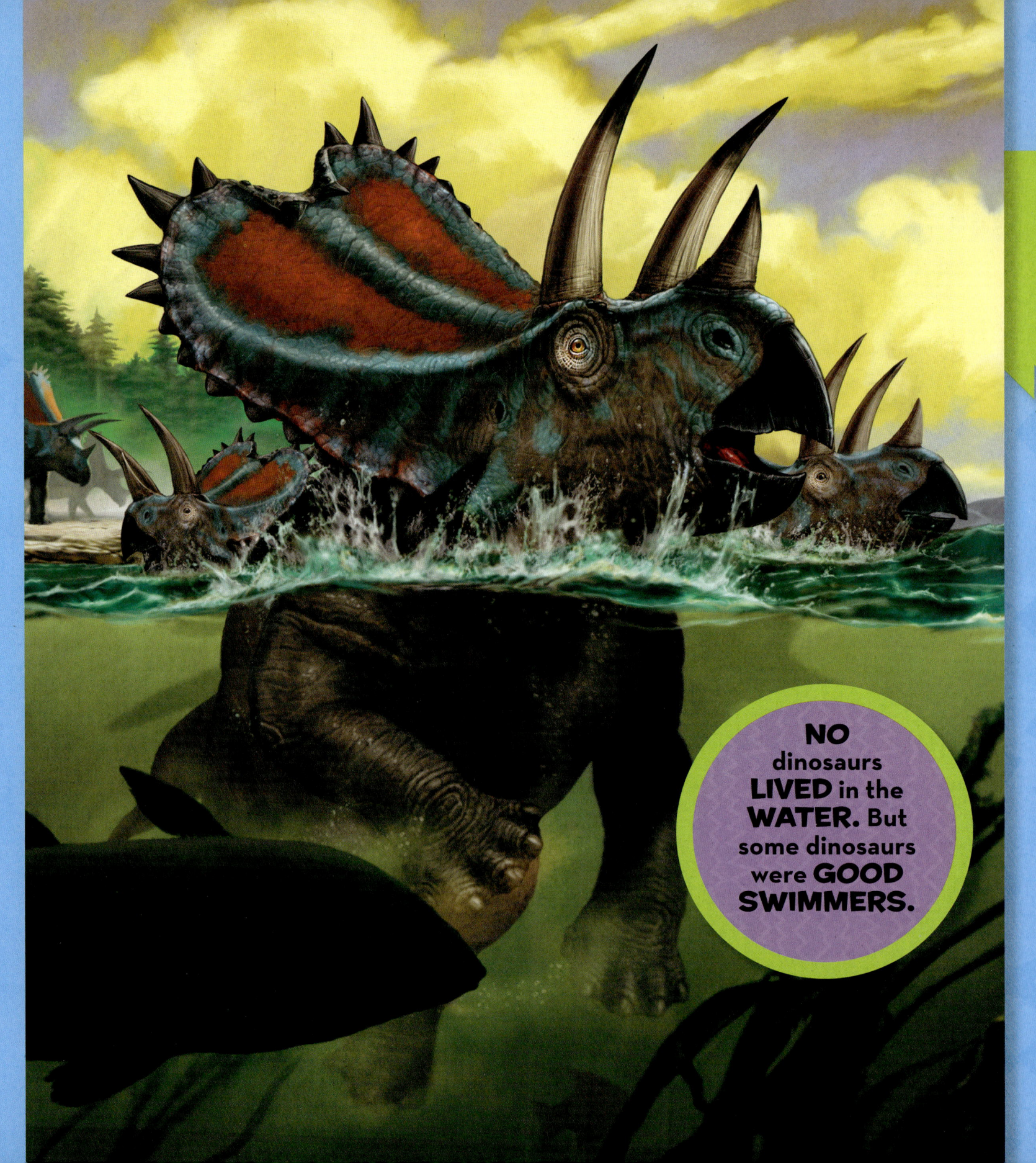

NO dinosaurs **LIVED** in the **WATER**. But some dinosaurs were **GOOD SWIMMERS**.

BIG

PENTACERATOPS HAD A HORNED HEAD.

This dinosaur had five horns on its head. Two stood over its eyes. Two stuck out from its cheeks. The fifth horn grew on top of its nose.

A frill stretched around the back of its head. Short spikes grew all along the frill. The frill helped the dinosaur show off to other *Pentaceratops*.

FACTS

WHEN IT LIVED
late Cretaceous

FOOD
plants

SIZE

Do you like to swim?

SAY MY NAME: PEN-ta-SER-ah-tops

BIG

HERRERASAURUS HAD A BIG MOUTH.

Herrerasaurus **WALKED** on its **HIND LEGS.**

This fierce meat-eater could open its mouth very wide. Its strong jaws slid back and forth and chomped down hard. Its big mouth held a lot of strong teeth.

Herrerasaurus was one of the earliest big meat-eaters. It lived in the Triassic, the beginning of the time of dinosaurs.

FACTS

WHEN IT LIVED
late Triassic

FOOD
meat

SIZE

SAY MY NAME: huh-RARE-ah-SORE-us

Herrerasaurus used its **TEETH** to cut prey into **CHUNKS** it could **SWALLOW**.

What do you use your teeth for?

Does the horn on this dinosaur's nose remind you of a rhinoceros?

BIG

STYRACOSAURUS HAD A FANCY FACE.

Styracosaurus used its **SHARP BEAK** to **CHOP OFF** the **PLANTS** it ate.

A big horn on its nose, spikes along its frill, and knobs on its cheeks gave this dinosaur an unusual look.

Paleontologists have found many fossil skeletons of these dinosaurs together. They think *Styracosaurus* traveled in groups.

FACTS

WHEN IT LIVED
late Cretaceous

FOOD
plants

SIZE

SAY MY NAME: sty-RACK-oh-SORE-us

BIG

UTAHRAPTOR HAD CLAWED FEET.

Utahraptor had **POWERFUL LEGS.**

This dinosaur had scary-looking feet! When *Utahraptor* attacked, it leaped up in the air. Then it kicked hard. The big sharp claws on its feet stabbed its prey.

The claws on its feet were about 12 inches (30 centimeters) long. That is longer than the cover of this book.

Utahraptor also had a lot of sharp teeth. Like many small meat-eaters, this dinosaur was smart, fast, and dangerous.

FACTS

WHEN IT LIVED early Cretaceous

FOOD meat

SIZE

SAY MY NAME: YOO-tah-RAP-tore

Can you jump and kick like *Utahraptor*? Try it outside.

Paleontologists found this **DINOSAUR'S FOSSILS** in **UTAH**, in the United States. That is how it **GOT THE NAME** *Utahraptor*.

ANTARCTICA is a very COLD PLACE TODAY. But when *Cryolophosaurus* lived there, Antarctica **WAS MUCH WARMER.**

BIG

CRYOLOPHOSAURUS HAD A PRETTY CREST.

The crest on the top of *Cryolophosaurus*'s head was bony. Two little horns grew on each side. The decoration may have made the dinosaur attractive to other *Cryolophosaurus*.

What do you do to make yourself look nice for a party?

Paleontologists found this toothy dinosaur's fossils near the South Pole. It is one of the first dinosaurs to be discovered on the continent of Antarctica.

FACTS
WHEN IT LIVED
early Jurassic
FOOD
meat
SIZE

SAY MY NAME: CRY-oh-LOW-fo-SORE-us

BIG

NOTHRONYCHUS HAD CLAWED ARMS.

FACTS

WHEN IT LIVED
middle Cretaceous

FOOD
plants

SIZE

This plant-eater had huge claws on its hands. It used these claws to grab branches. *Nothronychus* had a beak and more than 100 tiny teeth.

You can see a giant relative of *Nothronychus* called *Therizinosaurus,* on page 90. They lived at different times and in different places.

There are at least **1,000 SPECIES** of dinosaurs.

SAY MY NAME: noh-THRON-ih-cuss

Can you point to the bird flying in the forest near the dinosaur?

Triceratops had about **800 SMALL TEETH.** The plant-eater used them to **CUT UP** the **TOUGH PLANTS** it ate.

FACTS

WHEN IT LIVED
late Cretaceous

FOOD
plants

SIZE

BIG

TRICERATOPS HAD THREE HORNS.

The horns on its head and the frill around its neck were used to show off to other *Triceratops*. The dinosaurs sometimes used their horns to fight each other, too.

Triceratops means "THREE-HORNED FACE."

Paleontologists found the fossils of three young *Triceratops* together. This makes them think that these dinosaurs traveled in family groups.

Can you point to the three horns on this *Triceratops* fossil?

SAY MY NAME: tri-SERR-ah-tops

BIG

MUTTABURRASAURUS HAD A BUMPY NOSE.

No one knows exactly why *Muttaburrasaurus* had a big bump on its skull. It was right behind the holes in its nose, called nostrils.

Here are three hypotheses about this dinosaur's odd nose.

Scientists often make a **GOOD GUESS**, called a **HYPOTHESIS**, to answer things they do not know for sure.

It might have helped *Muttaburrasaurus* smell things better, look more attractive to a mate, or make its calls louder.

FACTS

WHEN IT LIVED
early Cretaceous

FOOD
plants

SIZE

SAY MY NAME: mutt-ah-BUHR-ah-SORE-us

Nobody knows for sure what **SOUNDS DINOSAURS MADE.**

What is your hypothesis about what this dinosaur sounded like?

FOSSILS of *Europasaurus* were **FOUND** in **GERMANY**, a country on the continent of **EUROPE.**

BIG

EUROPASAURUS WAS AN ISLAND DINO.

This dinosaur was smaller than its relatives. *Europasaurus* is closely related to *Apatosaurus* (see page 106) and *Brachiosaurus* (see page 108).

Europasaurus looked a lot like those gigantic dinosaurs, but it did not grow as big. It lived in forests on islands, small bits of land surrounded by water.

FACTS

WHEN IT LIVED
late Jurassic

FOOD
plants

SIZE

Can you draw a picture of an island?

SAY MY NAME: yoo-ROPE-ah-SORE-us

BIG

OURANOSAURUS HAD A BACK SAIL.

The **BIG CREST** along this dinosaur's whole back looked a bit like the **SAIL** on a **SAILBOAT**.

Ouranosaurus lived in a rainy place where the land often flooded.

The dinosaur had plenty of plants to eat. But when the land flooded, *Ouranosaurus* had to watch out for gigantic crocodiles, which lived in the time of dinosaurs.

Have you ever seen a crocodile at the zoo?

SAY MY NAME: oo-RAHN-oh-SORE-us

FACTS

WHEN IT LIVED
early Cretaceous

FOOD
plants

SIZE

Can you see better with one eye open or with both eyes open?

BIG

CARNOTAURUS HAD A SQUARE HEAD.

This dinosaur might remind you of a bull because it had two horns on its head. The odd-looking dinosaur had a very small lower jaw. Its head was shaped like a square.

Some dinosaurs couldn't see in front of them with both eyes at the same time. But *Carnotaurus*'s eyes were far enough forward on its face that it could see ahead with both eyes at once.

Carnotaurus had **TINY ARMS.** They were so small that the **MEAT-EATER** could not use them to do much.

FACTS

WHEN IT LIVED
late Cretaceous

FOOD
meat

SIZE

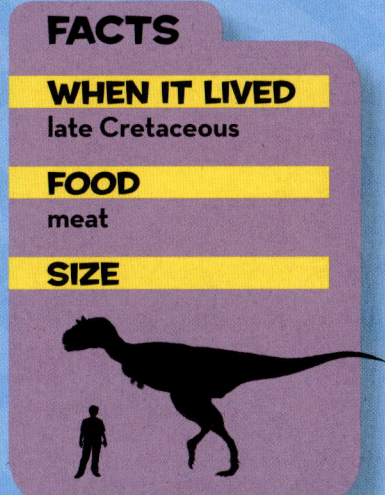

SAY MY NAME: KAR-no-TORE-us

BIG

STEGOSAURUS HAD A SPIKED TAIL.

Huge spikes on *Stegosaurus*'s tail were a good weapon. If a predator threatened it, *Stegosaurus* could swing its big tail and smack the enemy with the spikes.

Stegosaurus was the **BIGGEST SPECIES** of plate-backed plant-eaters.

Stegosaurus also had tall plates sticking up from its back. Another dinosaur in this book had tall plates, too. Do you remember *Huayangosaurus* on page 36?

FACTS
WHEN IT LIVED
late Jurassic
FOOD
plants
SIZE

SAY MY NAME: STEG-oh-SORE-us

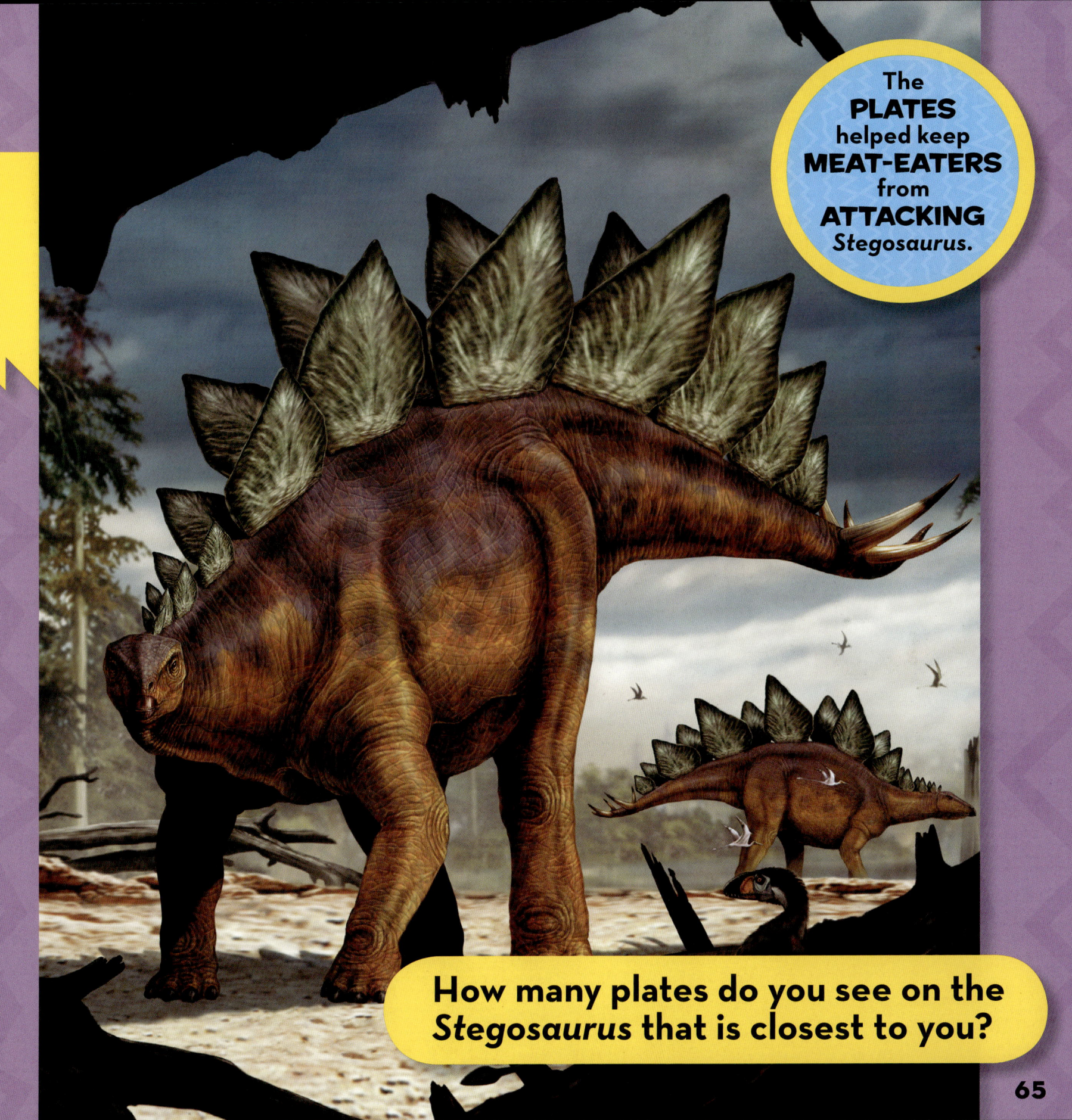

The **PLATES** helped keep **MEAT-EATERS** from **ATTACKING** *Stegosaurus*.

How many plates do you see on the *Stegosaurus* that is closest to you?

BIG

CORYTHOSAURUS HAD A HELMET HEAD.

Corythosaurus was one of several related species of dinosaurs called crested duckbills.

These dinosaurs lived in **GROUPS** called **HERDS.**

FACTS
WHEN IT LIVED late Cretaceous
FOOD plants
SIZE

When *Corythosaurus* breathed in, the air traveled from its nose up through the crest on its head. Its crest may have made the dinosaur's sounds louder.

Do you have a soft voice and a loud voice? Say "Corythosaurus" both ways!

SAY MY NAME: co-RITH-oh-SORE-us

BIG

PLATEOSAURUS WAS A LEAF CHOMPER.

Paleontologists have **FOUND** more than **100 SKELETONS** of this kind of dinosaur.

At the time *Plateosaurus* lived, it was one of the biggest dinosaurs.

It had a lot of teeth for ripping leaves off trees.

If *Plateosaurus* wanted to eat leaves that were high in a tree, the dinosaur could stand on its hind legs to reach them. It may have used its arms to pull down branches.

SAY MY NAME: PLAT-ee-oh-SORE-us

FACTS

WHEN IT LIVED
late Triassic

FOOD
plants

SIZE

What do you do if you can't reach something you want?

Sometimes dinosaurs **FOUGHT EACH OTHER** to see which one was **STRONGER.**

70

BIG

PACHYCEPHALOSAURUS HAD A THICK HEAD.

Pachycephalosaurus had a very hard head. These dinosaurs may have used their heads to whack each other's sides.

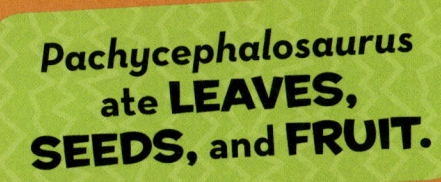
Pachycephalosaurus ate **LEAVES**, **SEEDS**, and **FRUIT**.

Some dinosaurs fought each other to guard the area where they wanted to live. They did not always like to share their space.

FACTS

WHEN IT LIVED
late Cretaceous

FOOD
plants

SIZE

Can you name three things that you are good about sharing?

SAY MY NAME: pack-ee-SEF-ah-lo-SORE-us

IN THIS CHAPTER YOU WILL READ ABOUT 14 GIANT DINOSAURS.

SMALL
up to 15 feet long
(5 meters)

BIG
15 to 30 feet long
(5 to 10 meters)

GIANT
30 to 65 feet long
(10 to 25 meters)

GIGANTIC
more than 65 feet long
(25 meters)

Tyrannosaurus
(See pages 100 and 101.)

GIANT

Mother *Maiasaura* **BROUGHT FOOD** to their **BABIES** while they were still **IN THE NEST.**

GIANT

MAIASAURA WAS A GOOD MOTHER.

Like all dinosaurs, *Maiasaura* laid eggs. Most meat-eaters' eggs were long and thin. Plant-eaters like *Maiasaura* laid rounder eggs.

These dinosaurs were too big to sit on their eggs to keep them warm. Instead, *Maiasaura* mothers covered their eggs with leaves.

FACTS
WHEN IT LIVED
late Cretaceous

FOOD
plants

SIZE

Where do your mom and dad get food to bring home?

SAY MY NAME: MA-ya-SORE-a

GIANT

IGUANODON HAD SPIKED HANDS.

Iguanodon had spikes on its hands. The spikes were in the place where thumbs might be, but were actually part of the dinosaur's wrist bones.

Iguanodon may have used its "thumbs" to stab a predator if it attacked.

FACTS

WHEN IT LIVED
early Cretaceous

FOOD
plants

SIZE

What do your thumbs help you do?

Iguanodon had three **STRONG FINGERS** and a **LONG LITTLE** finger.

SAY MY NAME: ig-WAN-oh-don

The first **FLOWERING PLANTS** appeared at about the same time that *Iguanodon* lived.

The **TAIL** of the *Ankylosaurus* had a **HARD, BONY CLUB** on the end of it.

If you were an *Ankylosaurus*, would you rather face a giant crocodile or a *Tyrannosaurus*?

GIANT

ANKYLOSAURUS HAD AN ARMORED BODY.

Ankylosaurus had a strong body covered in tough armor. This dinosaur moved slowly. It did not run away from trouble. It depended on its hard body for protection. Even its eyelids were covered with armor.

A *Tyrannosaurus,* such as the one in the picture at left, would have had a hard time biting the armored *Ankylosaurus.* (You can read more about *Tyrannosaurus* on page 100.)

SAY MY NAME: AN-kee-lo-SORE-us

When facing an **ENEMY** such as a giant crocodile, *Ankylosaurus* could use its **HEAVY TAIL** to **HIT** the **ATTACKER**.

FACTS

WHEN IT LIVED
late Cretaceous

FOOD
plants

SIZE

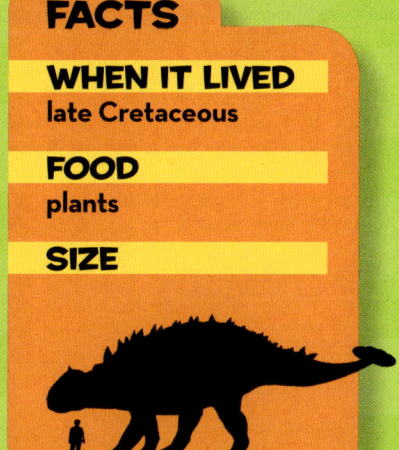

GIANT

TSINTAOSAURUS HAD A UNICORN SKULL.

Tsintaosaurus had a long bone that stuck out from its forehead, making it look a bit like a unicorn. But unicorns are make-believe. *Tsintaosaurus* was real.

Can you think of other make-believe creatures?

Paleontologists had to find more than one fossil skull before they were convinced that the long bone really grew from the dinosaur's forehead.

FACTS

WHEN IT LIVED
late Cretaceous

FOOD
plants

SIZE

SAY MY NAME: sin-tau-SORE-us

Tsintaosaurus **HORNS** may have been a **DECORATION** that made the dinosaurs attractive to each other.

Can you name some healthy green things that you eat?

GIANT

LESSEMSAURUS WAS A BIG EATER.

Big dinosaurs ate big meals. *Lessemsaurus* had to eat a lot of plants like the cycads it is eating in the picture.

As you know, there are no more dinosaurs like *Lessemsaurus*. But did you know that there were dinosaurs on Earth for about 160,000,000 (160 million) years?

That is such a long time it is almost impossible to imagine!

SAY MY NAME: LES-em-SORE-us

FACTS

WHEN IT LIVED
late Triassic

FOOD
plants

SIZE

Lessemsaurus was named for **DINO EXPERT** Don Lessem, who has written more than 40 books about dinosaurs.

GIANT

AMARGASAURUS HAD A NECK SAIL.

Amargasaurus may have used its **LONG TAIL** like a **WHIP** to **PROTECT** itself from attackers.

This dinosaur's long neck and back were decorated with what looked like a sail. Stiff spines held up *Amargasaurus*'s sail.

No one knows for sure why *Amargasaurus* had the big sail. It might have scared away enemies. Or it may have helped keep the big animal cool.

FACTS

WHEN IT LIVED
early Cretaceous

FOOD
plants

SIZE

SAY MY NAME: uh-MARG-uh-SORE-us

84

Some of the **SPINES** on the *Amargasaurus* were as **TALL AS A TEN-YEAR-OLD.**

How many dinosaurs do you see in the picture?

GIANT

RIOJASAURUS WAS THE FIRST GIANT DINO.

This giant dinosaur was one of the first really big plant-eaters. It had a long, thin neck and tail. Its body and legs were heavy.

Smaller dinosaurs could walk on two legs. But *Riojasaurus* walked on all four legs. The giant and gigantic dinosaurs had to walk on four legs because two legs could not hold up all their weight.

Many dinosaur **NAMES** end in *"saurus."* **SAURUS** means **LIZARD**.

FACTS

WHEN IT LIVED
late Triassic

FOOD
plants

SIZE

SAY MY NAME: REE-oh-hah-SORE-us

GIANT

YANGCHUANOSAURUS WAS A SCARY DINO.

Yangchuanosaurus was so powerful it could kill prey much larger than itself.

One of the dinosaurs that had to watch out for this meat-eater was the gigantic *Mamenchisaurus,* which you can see on page 111. The two dinosaurs lived in the same place at the same time.

A construction **WORKER** in **CHINA** found the first skeleton of *Yangchuanosaurus* while digging to **BUILD A DAM.**

FACTS

WHEN IT LIVED
late Jurassic

FOOD
meat

SIZE

Do you think this dinosaur looks scary?

SAY MY NAME: YANG-chew-an-oh-SORE-us

BIG TEETH and BIG CLAWS made *Yangchuanosaurus* a GREAT PREDATOR.

Therizinosaurus's **CLAWS** were **THREE FEET LONG.** That's a little longer than three copies of this book side by side!

GIANT

THERIZINOSAURUS HAD HUGE CLAWS.

Even though this dinosaur had huge claws, *Therizinosaurus* was not a meat-eating predator. It was a plant-eater.

It also may have eaten insects such as ants and beetles. Its big claws would have been handy for digging in the ground to find insects.

FACTS

WHEN IT LIVED
late Cretaceous

FOOD
plants and insects

SIZE

> Have you ever tried digging in dirt to find an earthworm?

SAY MY NAME: THERE-ih-ZIN-oh-SORE-us

GIANT

ACROCANTHOSAURUS HAD EYE RIDGES.

Acrocanthosaurus had **38 SHARP TEETH** in its upper jaw.

Acrocanthosaurus peered out of eyes that had bony ridges around them.

This dinosaur had very strong muscles in its neck and back.

Acrocanthosaurus was one of the biggest meat-eating dinosaurs. It was not a fast runner. But it was powerful and could kill prey bigger than itself.

FACTS

WHEN IT LIVED
early Cretaceous

FOOD
meat

SIZE

SAY MY NAME: ACK-ro-CAN-tho-SORE-us

Acrocanthosaurus **HUNTED** other kinds of dinosaurs, like the one in the background, for **DINNER!**

If you were a dinosaur, would you rather be a plant-eater or a meat-eater?

The **SPINES** on *Spinosaurus's* back reached **SEVEN FEET HIGH**—taller than almost any human.

How many pterosaurs do you see flying in the sky in the picture?

GIANT

SPINOSAURUS HAD A LONG JAW.

Spinosaurus had a long jaw like a crocodile's. It caught fish to eat.

Do you remember *Amargasaurus* from page 84? It looked a little like *Spinosaurus*. They both had long spines and sails on their backs.

This dinosaur was a meat-eater; *Amargasaurus* was a plant-eater. The two dinosaurs didn't live at the same time. *Spinosaurus* lived later.

FACTS

WHEN IT LIVED
late Cretaceous

FOOD
meat

SIZE

SAY MY NAME: SPINE-oh-SORE-us

GIANT

EDMONTOSAURUS WAS A HERD TRAVELER.

Every year *Edmontosaurus* traveled long distances to find food. This kind of travel is called migration. *Edmontosaurus* migrated in large herds.

What is the farthest you have traveled from home?

Edmontosaurus herds walked more than **1,000 MILES** a year. It would take a whole day and night to go that far in a car.

Edmontosaurus had hundreds of diamond-shaped teeth. It used its teeth to grind the tough plants it ate.

SAY MY NAME: ed-MON-toh-SORE-us

FACTS

WHEN IT LIVED
late Cretaceous

FOOD
plants

SIZE

In this picture, pterosaurs **SWOOP UNDER** the *Shunosaurus*'s **LONG TAIL.**

GIANT

SHUNOSAURUS HAD A CLUB TAIL.

There was a bony lump on the end of *Shunosaurus*'s tail. The huge dinosaur could swing its tail and hit enemies with the hard end.

Can you name three animals you have seen that have tails?

Workers digging in China found the fossils of several entire *Shunosaurus* in one place. Finding a whole fossilized dinosaur is rare.

FACTS

WHEN IT LIVED
middle Jurassic

FOOD
plants

SIZE

SAY MY NAME: SHOO-noh-SORE-us

GIANT

TYRANNOSAURUS WAS THE DINOSAUR KING.

Tyrannosaurus is one of the most famous dinosaurs. It was a fierce hunter with long, sharp teeth.

The jaws of the *Tyrannosaurus* were very strong. The dinosaur could use its jaws to crush animals it caught for food.

FACTS

WHEN IT LIVED
late Cretaceous

FOOD
meat

SIZE

Can you think of another animal that is a fierce hunter?

Tyrannosaurus could have **GULPED** down some **SMALL DINOSAURS** without even chewing.

SAY MY NAME: tye-RAN-oh-SORE-us

Tyrannosaurus's **TEETH** were the size of **BANANAS.**

IN THIS CHAPTER YOU WILL READ ABOUT 8 GIGANTIC DINOSAURS.

SMALL
up to 15 feet long
(5 meters)

BIG
15 to 30 feet long
(5 to 10 meters)

GIANT
30 to 65 feet long
(10 to 25 meters)

GIGANTIC
more than 65 feet long
(25 meters)

Brachiosaurus
(See pages 108 and 109.)

GIGANTIC

103

This gigantic dinosaur **LIVED** in the **FOREST**.

GIGANTIC

REBBACHISAURUS WAS AN AFRICAN GIANT.

This gigantic dinosaur lived in Africa. It had a big ridge, or long bump, on its back.

The ridge may have helped the dinosaur cool off.

Fresh air and breezes could reach all the skin covering the long ridge. That could help a hot dino cool down!

The biggest dinosaurs were plant-eaters. They had **SMALL BRAINS** about the **SIZE** of two **CHICKEN EGGS**.

FACTS

WHEN IT LIVED
late Cretaceous

FOOD
plants

SIZE

How do you cool off when you get too hot?

SAY MY NAME: re-BASH-eh-SORE-us

105

GIGANTIC

APATOSAURUS WAS A GOOD PROTECTOR.

Long ago some paleontologists thought they had found the fossils of a new dinosaur. They named it *Brontosaurus*.

Years later, other paleontologists realized that the "*Brontosaurus*" fossils were really those of a dinosaur that already had a name: *Apatosaurus*.

So there never really was a dinosaur called *Brontosaurus*.

FACTS
WHEN IT LIVED late Jurassic
FOOD plants
SIZE

Did anyone ever call you by the wrong name?

SAY MY NAME: uh-PAT-uh-SORE-us

Traveling in herds, *Apatosaurus* may have protected **YOUNG DINOSAURS** by keeping them in the **MIDDLE OF THE GROUP.**

FACTS

WHEN IT LIVED
late Jurassic

FOOD
plants

SIZE

GIGANTIC

BRACHIOSAURUS WAS A TREETOP EATER.

Brachiosaurus had a very long neck. Its front legs were longer than its back legs.

The dinosaur's long neck and front legs helped it reach leaves growing high up in trees.

This tall dinosaur was **HEAVY**. It **WEIGHED** more than **12 ELEPHANTS**.

How much do you weigh?

Brachiosaurus walked very slowly and could not run.

SAY MY NAME: BRACK-ee-oh-SORE-us

GIGANTIC

MAMENCHISAURUS HAD A LONG NECK.

This dinosaur had the longest neck of any animal that ever lived. Its neck was as long as five or six giraffe necks!

Mamenchisaurus didn't have to walk around much to keep eating. It could stand in one spot and sweep its head back and forth to reach plenty of leaves.

FACTS
WHEN IT LIVED late Jurassic
FOOD plants
SIZE

Stretch your arm up a wall while standing on tiptoe. Who in your family can reach the highest?

SAY MY NAME: mah-MEHN-chee-SORE-us

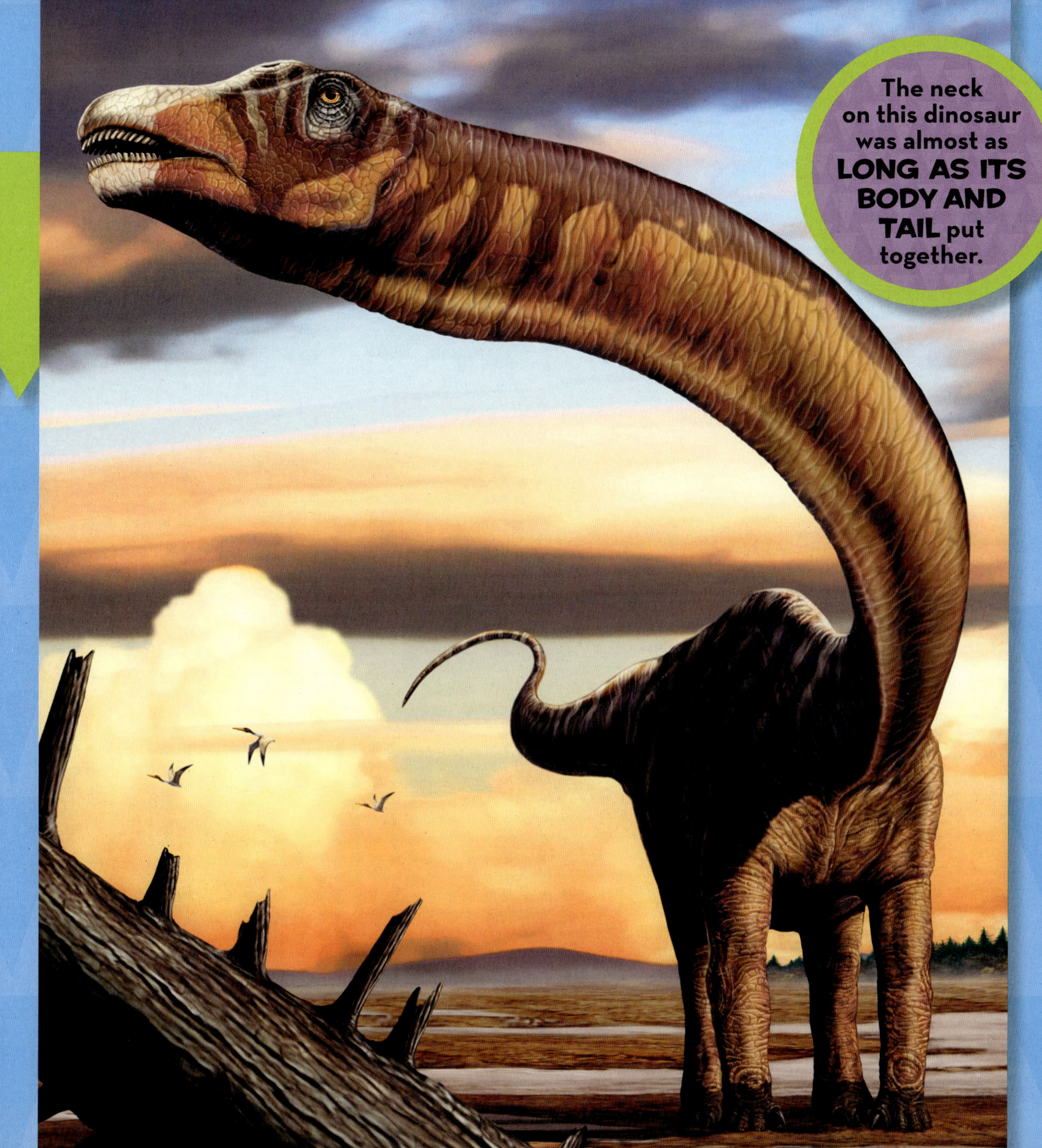

The neck on this dinosaur was almost as **LONG AS ITS BODY AND TAIL** put together.

Have you ever seen a dog wag its tail to show that it is happy?

GIGANTIC

DIPLODOCUS HAD A WHIPLIKE TAIL.

Diplodocus's tail was longer than any other dinosaur's.

Diplodocus had **LONG, SKINNY TEETH.**

FACTS

WHEN IT LIVED
late Jurassic

FOOD
plants

SIZE

Some paleontologists used to think that when it snapped its long tail like a whip, the noise scared away predators.

Now they think that *Diplodocus* actually used its tail to signal, or "talk" to, other dinosaurs.

SAY MY NAME: dih-PLOD-uh-kus

GIGANTIC

NUROSAURUS WAS A DESERT DISCOVERY.

The **FOSSIL SKELETON** of *Nurosaurus* was discovered in 1990.

Nurosaurus fossils were found in a desert in China. It was long and heavy—the biggest dinosaur in the area at the time it lived.

Dinosaurs disappeared about 65 million years ago. Scientists think that a big asteroid—a huge rock from space—hit the Earth. It made big clouds of dust and smoke that changed the weather, killing almost all the dinosaurs.

SAY MY NAME: NEW-ro-SORE-us

Have you ever been to a desert?

FACTS

WHEN IT LIVED
early Cretaceous

FOOD
plants

SIZE

There was only **ONE DINOSAUR** known to be **BIGGER** than *Paralititan*. You'll see it when you turn the page.

GIGANTIC

PARALITITAN WAS A MANGROVE DINO.

Paralititan lived in mangrove forests near the edge of an ocean. Mangroves are trees that grow where it is very wet. Mangrove forests are filled with these trees and many other plants.

Living there meant that this plant-eater had plenty to eat. It needed to eat hundreds of pounds of food every day.

FACTS

WHEN IT LIVED
late Cretaceous

FOOD
plants

SIZE

The **WET FOREST** where *Paralititan* lived millions of years ago is now a **HUGE DESERT**.

What is the biggest animal you have ever seen?

SAY MY NAME: pah-ral-e-TIE-tan

GIGANTIC

ARGENTINOSAURUS WAS A HEAVYWEIGHT.

Some dinosaurs were as long as this dinosaur. A few were taller. But *Argentinosaurus* may have been the heaviest. It weighed about the same as 20 elephants.

Araucarian **TREES**—which *Argentinosaurus* ate so long ago—**STILL GROW** in **ARGENTINA,** South America.

FACTS
WHEN IT LIVED
late Cretaceous
FOOD
plants
SIZE

Paleontologists have only found fossils of a few *Argentinosaurus* bones. But they know enough about dinosaurs to figure out what the whole dinosaur probably looked like.

SAY MY NAME: ahr-gen-TEEN-oh-SORE-us

Argentinosaurus was the **LARGEST** known animal that **EVER LIVED ON LAND.**

If you were a dinosaur, which dinosaur in this book would you want to be?

PARENT TIPS

Extend your child's experience beyond the pages of this book. A visit to a natural history museum's dinosaur exhibit is one great way to continue satisfying your child's curiosity about dinosaurs. Take this book along with you to see how many dinosaurs featured here are on exhibit at the museum. Here are some other activities you can do with *National Geographic Little Kids First Big Book of Dinosaurs*.

SIZE UP DINOSAURS (MATH)

The dinosaurs in this book are categorized according to size: small, big, giant, and gigantic. Compare the lengths of one dinosaur from each chapter to your child's length (lying down). Mark a starting line. Have your child lie down with her feet at the line. Mark her length. Then, from that same starting line, use a measuring tape and help her measure and mark the sizes of *Micropachycephalosaurus* (2 feet/.6 meters long), *Cryolophosaurus* (20 feet/6 meters long), *Riojasaurus* (36 feet/11 meters long), and *Diplodocus* (90 feet/27 meters long). Bonus idea: Have your child count how many of her lengths equal each dinosaur's length.

CREATE A TIME LINE (TIME)

"Millions of years ago" is a hard concept for adults to grasp, much less for kids who are learning to picture last year, this year, and next year. Have your child draw a simple time line to help him get a picture of the Triassic, Jurassic, and Cretaceous periods. Label Triassic at the left, Jurassic in the middle, and Cretaceous at the right. Draw an arrow on the right end of the line and label it so that it points to "today." Pointing to the line, explain that the Cretaceous was a long time ago (145 to 65 million years ago); the Jurassic was even longer ago (200 to 145 mya); and the Triassic was the longest ago (250 to 200 mya). Compare to yesterday, last week, and last month.

BUILD A HIDING PLACE (IMAGINATION)

Grab a couple of high-back chairs and a big bedsheet or blanket. Pretend that a time machine took you and your child back to the time of the dinosaurs. You're hidden from the dinosaurs inside a blind, so that you can make observations without being detected. Ask your child to tell you what she sees, then tell her what you see, and continue taking turns building a story about your time with the dinosaurs. When you've exhausted your imaginations, time-travel back to the present and draw pictures of what you saw.

DINOSAUR EGG HUNT (SEARCH STRATEGIES)

Make dinosaur eggs using papier-mâché (find directions online). Place a toy or treat inside each egg before sealing. Hide the eggs around the house or yard. Have your child invite a few friends over and have a dinosaur egg hunt. When the children find all the eggs, have them break the eggs open to find the treats.

NAME THAT DINO (ALPHABET)

Have your child write the alphabet down the side of a big sheet of paper. Then go through this book and have your child identify the first letter of each dinosaur's name. Have him make a check mark next to the corresponding letter on his alphabet. If he's still interested in the game, have him make up new dinosaur names that begin with each of the letters without a check mark.

WATCHING DINOSAURS (OBSERVING)

Birds, by some definitions, are dinosaurs (see page 28). Attract "dinosaurs" to your backyard by setting up a "dinosaur feeder" (bird feeder). Sit with your child and watch the birds (they tend to be most active in early morning and late afternoon). Make a chart that lists the most common visitors to your feeder along the side and the days of the week along the top. Each day, have your child mark off the species of living dinosaurs that stop by for a visit.

DINOSAUR DIET (CATEGORIZING)

Some dinosaurs were plant-eaters, others meat-eaters, and a few were omnivores. Have your child decide which dinosaur diet he wants for dinner. Take him to the grocery store to buy the ingredients for a plant (vegetarian) or omnivorous (meat and vegetables) meal. Let him pick from among fruits, vegetables, and meats as you discuss how fruits and vegetables grow and which animals different meats come from.

PARENT TIPS

DIGGING FOR DINOS (MOTOR SKILLS)
Pretend to be paleontologists digging for fossils. Using ten cleaned and boiled chicken bones, make a dinosaur dig at home. Bury the bones at various levels in dirt in the yard, in a sandbox, or in sand placed in a big container. Using a toy shovel and a couple different sizes of paintbrushes, have your child dig carefully to find the ten "fossils" you've buried.

MAKE A DINOSAUR (CRAFTS and SHAPES)
Using colored construction paper, cut out several shapes—squares, ovals, triangles, circles, and rectangles—of various sizes. Your child can make pictures of dinosaurs by gluing the shapes onto a sheet of construction paper. For example, use a big circle to make the body, rectangles as legs, two triangles as open jaws, and tiny triangles as teeth.

DINO JOKES (HUMOR)
Goofy jokes are great for giggles. Search online for dinosaur jokes or make up your own. Encourage your child to make up a few, too. Here are three to get you started:

Q: How can you tell there's an *Apatosaurus* in your refrigerator?
A: The door won't close!

Q: Which dinosaur could jump higher than a house?
A: All of them. Houses can't jump!

Q: What did *Triceratops* sit on?
A: Its tricera-bottom.

DINOSAUR GAMES (PLAY)
Play a variation of duck, duck, goose by having your child and his friends call out dinosaur names instead: e.g. *"Apatosaurus, Apatosaurus, Tyrannosaurus!"* Play a variation of tag by pretending that the person who is "it" is a meat-eating dinosaur and the other players are prey. Play hide-and-seek, pretending that the seeker is a hunter and the others are prey.

DINOSAURS ONLINE (BONUS MATERIAL)
Go online to print dinosaur cards! kids.nationalgeographic.com/kids/animals/creature feature/

DINOSAUR MAP

Use this world map to see where fossils of the dinosaurs in this book were found.

NORTH AMERICA
Scutellosaurus
Struthiomimus
Pentaceratops
Styracosaurus
Utahraptor
Nothronychus
Triceratops
Stegosaurus
Corythosaurus
Pachycephalosaurus
Maiasaura
Iguanodon
Ankylosaurus
Acrocanthosaurus
Edmontosaurus
Tyrannosaurus
Apatosaurus
Brachiosaurus
Diplodocus

SOUTH AMERICA
Buitreraptor
Herrerasaurus
Carnotaurus
Lessemsaurus
Amargasaurus
Riojasaurus
Argentinosaurus

ANTARCTICA
Cryolophosaurus

GLOSSARY

CLAW
a sharp nail on an animal's foot or hand that is usually curved and slender

CONTINENT
one of seven large land divisions on Earth: North America, South America, Europe, Asia, Africa, Australia, and Antarctica

CRETACEOUS
the period of time from 145 to 65 million years ago. Most dinosaurs were extinct at the end of this period.

DESERT
a dry area of land that receives ten inches or less of rain each year

DRAGONFLY
any of several species of large insect with a long, slender body and two pairs of narrow wings

EXTINCT
no longer existing

FANG
a long, sharp tooth

FLOOD
overflowing of a body of water such as a river that spills onto normally dry land

FOSSIL
a preserved part or trace of an ancient animal or plant

FRILL
a feature around the neck of an animal that was, in the case of dinosaurs, made of either bone or cartilage

HERD
a group of animals that live together

HYPOTHESIS
an unproven explanation or assumption that needs further investigation or testing

ISLAND
a piece of land that is surrounded by water and is smaller than a continent

JURASSIC
the period of time from 200 to 145 million years ago

MANGROVE
a tree with very long roots that is native to tropical coastlines

MIGRATE
to move from one place to another regularly

OMNIVORE
an animal that eats both meat and plants

OSTRICH
a big, fast, flightless bird that lives in Africa. It is the largest bird alive today.

PALEONTOLOGIST
a scientist who studies dinosaurs and other extinct animals and their habitats

PREDATOR
an animal that hunts other animals (prey) for food

PREY
an animal that a predator hunts and kills for food

PTEROSAUR
an extinct flying reptile

SKELETON
the stiff structure, made of bone or cartilage, that supports the body's soft tissues and organs

SOUTH POLE
the southernmost point on Earth, located on the continent of Antarctica

SPECIES
a category, or kind, of animal or plant

TRIASSIC
the period of time from 250 to 200 million years ago

INDEX

A
Acrocanthosaurus 92, **93,** 122
Activities, dinosaur 120–121
Africa
  as continent 124
  dinosaur fossils 123
  gigantic dinosaur 104, **105**
  ostriches 125
  see also Niger; South Africa
Alphabet game 120
Amargasaurus 84, **85,** 95, 122
Ankylosaurus **78,** 79, 122
Antarctica
  climate change 50
  as continent 124
  dinosaur fossils 51, 122
  see also South Pole
Apatosaurus 106, **107,** 122
  dinosaur game 121
  relatives 59
Araucarian trees 118
Archaeopteryx 28, **29,** 123
Archaeornithomimus 20, **21,** 123
Argentina
  araucarian trees 118
  dinosaur fossils 32
Argentinosaurus 118, **119,** 122
Armored dinosaurs 22, **23, 30,** 31, **78,** 79
Arms
  clawed 52, **53**
  feathered 16, **16, 17**
  tiny **62,** 63
Asia
  as continent 124
  dinosaur fossils 123
  see also China; Mongolia
Asteroid impact 114
Australia
  as continent 124
  dinosaur fossils 123

B
Baby dinosaurs **17, 74**
Back sail 60, **61**
Beaked dinosaurs **26,** 27, **46,** 47, 52, **53**
Beetles 24, **25,** 91
Big dinosaurs 40–71
Bird feeders 120
Birds
  evolution 28
  link with dinosaurs 28, 120
  observing 120
  see also Archaeopteryx; Ostriches
Brachiosaurus 59, **102–103, 108,** 109, 122
Brain size: gigantic dinosaurs 105
Brontosaurus. see *Apatosaurus*
Buitreraptor 32, **33,** 122
Burrows 35

C
Canada: dinosaur fossils 32
Cards, dinosaur 121
Carnotaurus **62,** 63, 122
Cartilage 124, 125
China: dinosaur fossils 32, 88, 99, 114
Claw: definition 124
Claws, dinosaur
  for catching prey 25, 48, 89, 91
  clawed arms 52, **53**
  clawed feet 48, **49**
  for climbing 11, 24
  for defense 32
Compsognathus **18,** 19, 123
Continent: definition 124
Corythosaurus **66,** 67, 122
Crested
  duckbills 67
Cretaceous period
  definition 124
  time-line activity 120
Crocodiles, giant 60, 78, 79

Cryolophosaurus **50,** 51, 120, 122
Cycads 82, 83

D
Deserts 27, 114, 115, 117, 124
Dinosaurs
  colors 35
  diets 20, 120
  eggs 16, 75
  extinction 114, 124
  fighting 55, **70,** 71
  herds 67, 96, 107
  life spans 22
  nests 16, **17, 74**
  new species 81
  number of species 52
  sounds made by 57, 67
  vision 63
Diplodocus **112,** 113, 120, 122
Dragonflies 10, 18, 124

E
Earth
  asteroid impact 114
  continents 124
  southernmost point 125
  time of dinosaurs 8, 27, 83
Edmontosaurus 96, **97,** 122
Egg hunt, dinosaur 120
Europasaurus **58,** 59, 123
Europe
  as continent 124
  dinosaur fossils 123
  see also Germany
Extinct: definition 124

Eye ridges 92, **93**
Eyelids, armored 79
Eyes **34,** 35, 62, 63

F
Fangs **14,** 124
Feathers **10,** 11, **16, 17,** 24
Feet, clawed **48,** 49
Floods and flooding 60, 124
Flowering plants, first 77
Flying reptiles. see Pterosaurs
Footprints 26
Fossil: definition 124
Fossil-hunting game 121
Frill: definition 124
Frills, dinosaur **42,** 43, **46,** 47, **54,** 55
Fruit: as food for dinosaurs 20, 31, 71

G
Games, dinosaur 120-121
Germany: dinosaur fossils 58
Giant dinosaurs 72-100
Gigantic dinosaurs 102-119
Gliding dinosaurs 10, 11, 24, **25,** 28, **29**
Glossary 124-125

H
Heads, dinosaur
   helmet **66,** 67
   horned **42,** 43
   square **62,** 63
   thick **70,** 71
Heavy dinosaurs 87, 109, 114, 118
Herd: definition 124
Herrerasaurus 44, **45,** 122
Heterodontosaurus **14,** 15, 123
Huayangosaurus 36, **37,** 64, 123
Hypotheses 56, 57, 124

I
Iguanodon 76, **77,** 122, 123
Insects
   as prey of dinosaurs 19, 24, 32, 33, 91
   see also Beetles; Dragonflies
Islands 59, 124

J
Jokes, dinosaur 121
Jurassic period
   definition 124
   time-line activity 120

L
Leaellynasaura **34,** 35, 123
Lessem, Don 83
Lessemsaurus **82,** 83, 122
Lizards 17, 19, 32, 39, **86**
Long-necked dinosaurs 38, 39, 84, **85, 86,** 87, 108, **109,** 110, **111**

M
Maiasaura **74,** 75, 122
Make-believe creatures 80
Mamenchisaurus 88, 110, **111,** 123
Mangroves
   definition 124
   forests 117
Map 122-123
Math activity 120
Micropachycephalosaurus 12, **13,** 120, 123
Microraptor **10,** 11, 123
Migration 96, 124
Minmi **30,** 31, 123
Mongolia: dinosaur fossils 32
Motor skills: fossil dig 121
Museums, natural history 120
Muttaburrasaurus 56, **57,** 123

N
Neck sail **84,** 85
Niger: dinosaur fossils 32
North America
   as continent 124
   dinosaur fossils 122
   see also Canada; United States
Nostrils 56
Nothronychus 52, **53,** 122
Nurosaurus 114, **115,** 123

O
Omnivores 20, 39, 120, 124
Online resources 121
Ostriches 38, 125
Ouranosaurus 60, **61,** 123
Oviraptor 16, **16, 17,** 123

P
Pachycephalosaurus **70,** 71, 122
Paleontologist: definition 125
Paralititan **116,** 117, 123
Parent tips 120-121
Pentaceratops **42,** 43, 122

Plants
   araucarian trees 118
   cycads **82,** 83
   flowering plants **77**
   mangroves 117, 124
Plate-backed plant-eaters 36, 64
Plateosaurus 68, **69,** 123
Predators and prey
   definitions 19, 125
   dinosaur game 121
Psittacosaurus **26,** 27, 123
Pterosaurs **37, 94, 98,** 125

R
Rebbachisaurus **104,** 105, 123
Riojasaurus **86,** 87, 120, 122
Runners, fast 20-21, 38-39

S
Scansoriopteryx **8, 9,** 24, **25,** 123
Scutellosaurus **22,** 23, 122
Shunosaurus **98,** 99, 123
Signals, tail 112, 113
Skeleton: definition 125
Small dinosaurs 8-39
South Africa: dinosaur fossils 32
South America
   as continent 124
   dinosaur fossils 122
   see also Argentina
South Pole 35, 51, 125
Species: definition 125
Spiked hands **76,** 77
Spiked tail 64, **65**
Spiky back **36,** 37
Spines 84, 85, **94,** 95
Spinosaurus **94,** 95, 123
Stegosaurus 64, **65,** 122
Struthiomimus **38,** 39, 122
Styracosaurus **46,** 47, 122

T
Tails, dinosaur
   club **78, 98,** 99
   spiked 64, **65**
   whiplike 84, **112,** 113
Therizinosaurus 52, **90,** 91, 123
Time-line activity 120
Time-machine game 120
Triassic period
   definition 125
   time-line activity 120
Triceratops **40-41, 54,** 55, 121, 122
Tsintaosaurus 80, **81,** 123
Tyrannosaurus **72-73, 78,** 79, 100, **101,** 122
   dinosaur game 121

U
Unicorns 80
United States: dinosaur fossils 32, 49
Utah 49
Utahraptor **48,** 49, 122

W
World map 122-123
Wrist bones 76

Y
Yangchuanosaurus 88, **89,** 123

Prepared by the Book Division

Nancy Laties Feresten,
Senior Vice President, Editor in Chief, Children's Books

Jonathan Halling,
Design Director, Books and Children's Publishing

Jay Sumner,
Director of Photography, Children's Publishing

Jennifer Emmett,
Editorial Director, Children's Books

Carl Mehler,
Director of Maps

R. Gary Colbert,
Production Director

Jennifer A. Thornton,
Managing Editor

Staff for This Book

Robin Terry, *Project Manager*
Catherine D. Hughes, *Project Editor*
David M. Seager, *Art Director*
Lori Epstein, *Senior Illustrations Editor*
Ruthie Thompson, *Designer*
Wanda Jones, Ph.D., *Research*
Kate Olesin, *Editorial Assistant*
Kathryn Robbins, *Design Production Assistant*
Hillary Moloney, *Illustrations Assistant*
Grace Hill, *Associate Managing Editor*
Lewis R. Bassford, *Production Manager*
Susan Borke, *Legal and Business Affairs*

Manufacturing and Quality Management

Christopher A. Liedel, *Chief Financial Officer*
Phillip L. Schlosser, *Senior Vice President*
Chris Brown, *Technical Director*
Nicole Elliott, *Manager*
Rachel Faulise, *Manager*
Robert L. Barr, *Manager*

For Jack and Christopher, the loves of my life, and for little kids everywhere, whose perpetual curiosity inspires me every day. A special thanks to Stephanie Hughes, Aline Alexander Newman, Mary Ann Teitelbaum, and Jennifer Kirkpatrick Zicht for their invaluable help with this book. —C.D.H.

A special thanks to paleontologist Rodolfo Coria, Ph.D., of Neuquén, Argentina, for being so generous with his time and expertise in the creation of this book.

Acknowledgments

Matthew F. Bonnan, Ph.D., Dept. of Biological Sciences, Western Illinois University
Brooks B. Britt, Dept. of Geology, Brigham Young University
Robin Cuthbertson, University of Calgary
Andrew A. Farke, Ph.D., Curator of Paleontology, Raymond M. Alf Museum of Paleontology
Catherine A. Forster, Ph.D., Dept. of Biological Sciences, The George Washington University
Thomas R. Holtz, Jr., Ph.D., Dept. of Geology, University of Maryland
Dr. John "Jack" Horner, Curator of Paleontology, Museum of the Rockies
James I. Kirkland, Ph.D., Utah Geological Survey
Kevin Padian, Ph.D., Museum of Paleontology, University of California, Berkeley
Thomas H. Rich, Ph.D., Curator of Vertebrate Paleontology, Museum Victoria
Alex Tirabasso, Canadian Museum of Nature
John A. Whitlock, Ph.D., University of Michigan Museum of Paleontology
Xu Xing, Ph.D., Institute of Vertebrate Paleontology and Paleoanthropology, Chinese Academy of Sciences
Professor Fucheng Zhang, Institute of Vertebrate Paleontology and Paleoanthropology, Chinese Academy of Sciences

Photo Credits
p. 55, Francois Gohier/Photo Researchers Inc.; p. 68, Mervyn Rees/Alamy

Published by Collins
An imprint of HarperCollins Publishers
1 Robroyston Gate,
Glasgow
G33 1JN
www.harpercollins.co.uk

HarperCollins Publishers
Macken House, 39/40 Mayor Street Upper, Dublin 1
D01 C9W8 Ireland

© 2011 National Geographic Partners LLC. All rights reserved. NATIONAL GEOGRAPHIC KIDS and Yellow Border Design are trademarks of National Geographic Society, used under license.

First published 2011
This edition 2026

ISBN 9780008825294

10 9 8 7 6 5 4 3 2 1

All rights reserved. No part of this publication may be reproduced, stored in a retrieval system, or transmitted, in any form or by any means, electronic, mechanical, photocopying, recording or otherwise without the prior permission in writing of the publisher and copyright owners. Without limiting the exclusive rights of any author, contributor or the publisher of this publication, any unauthorised use of this publication to train generative artificial intelligence (AI) technologies is expressly prohibited.

HarperCollins also exercise their rights under Article 4(3) of the Digital Single Market Directive 2019/790 and expressly reserve this publication from the text and data mining exception.

The contents of this publication are believed correct at the time of printing. Nevertheless the publisher can accept no responsibility for errors or omissions, changes in the detail given or for any expense or loss thereby caused.

HarperCollins does not warrant that any website mentioned in this title will be provided uninterrupted, that any website will be error free, that defects will be corrected, or that the website or the server that makes it available are free of viruses or bugs. For full terms and conditions please refer to the site terms provided on the website.

A catalogue record for this book is available from the British Library

Printed in India

If you would like to comment on any aspect of this book, please contact us at the above address or online.
natgeokidsbooks.co.uk
collins.reference@harpercollins.co.uk

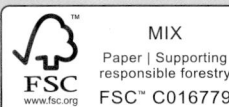

MIX
Paper | Supporting responsible forestry
FSC
www.fsc.org
FSC™ C016779